MW00979322

Editor
Nicole Lagneau
Picture Research
Janice Croot
Production
Rosemary Bishop
Consultant
Arthur Rowe Warden ILEA
Religious Education Centre
Teacher Panel
Robin Pooley
Jane Rickell
Graham Tarrant
Illustrators
Geoffrey Beitz
John Bilham
Carole Gosheron

First published 1981
Macdonald Educational
Limited, Holywell House,
Worship Street,
London EC2A 2EN

© Macdonald Educational
Limited 1981

Published in the United States
by Silver Burdett Company,
Morristown, N.J.
1982 Printing

ISBN 0-382-06677-4
Library of Congress
Catalog Card No. 82-50627

Photographic credits
Barnaby's Picture Library
25, 32, 43; Bildhuset 19;
Camera Press 24, 29, 30;
Explorer/Fournier 6;
Robert Harding Associates
7; Alan Hutchison 17
(top), 18, 38, 40, 41;
National Gallery, London
26; Orion Press contents,
39; Popperfoto 20; Rex
Features 15, 31; Scottish
Tourist Board 15 (top);
Spectrum Colour Library
27; John Topham
Library 33; Trevor Wood
17 (bottom); Zefa/Studio
Benser 11; W. Braun
cover 21.

*Cover: A Japanese
festival.*

Festivals

Jeanne McFarland

Silver Burdett Company

Contents

How to use this book
This book tells you all about festivals, and the things people celebrate. It describes seasonal festivals, folk festivals and different kinds of religious festivals. Look first at the contents page to see if the subject you want is listed. For instance if you want to find out about Hindu festivals, you will find them described on pages 34 and 35. The index will tell you how many times a particular subject is mentioned, and whether there is a picture of it. A Christmas tree for instance is mentioned on page 28. The glossary explains the more difficult words.

Rituals

All over the world people have many different customs and faiths, but at some time or other during the year they set aside a special occasion to get together and have a feast or festival.

Throughout the ages, people have celebrated the changing seasons, honoured their gods, or simply shared the experience of important events in their lives.

Seasons

The rhythm of the seasons was a fascinating mystery for our ancestors. Early people believed that spirits controlled the rising and setting of the sun. When the sun shone, the grass grew, the animals became fat for the hunt, and the trees blossomed. Winter was a very worrying time; the earth seemed to sleep.

The spirits or gods had to be honoured and worshipped if they were to continue to provide warmth, light and food. So early people shouted at the skies, painted themselves and dressed up to attract the attention of the gods. They offered *sacrifices* to them in the hope of a good hunting season.

Ritual

The chants and noise and all the preparations became formal rites repeated at regular intervals. Festivals today also require some kind of rituals, religious or *pagan*. Festivals are usually happy times: people may dress up, exchange gifts, dance, sing, and share food. If it is a religious occasion, there may be prayers and processions.

Symbol and tradition

The acts or rites which take place during a festival are often a simple way of representing an important event—a *symbol* of it. The lighting of a fire during a summer festival might represent the return of the summer sun. This kind of action is called symbolic.

Many of the seasonal festivals we have today were celebrated in the past. In some cultures, religious beliefs and seasonal rhythms go together.

In Mali, dancers wear animal masks as part of a ritual to ensure a good hunt. ▶

People gather every year at Stonehenge in the South of England to celebrate the rising of the sun on midsummer day. For early people, the stones may have been temples to the sun and sky. ▼

Ancient Egypt

The earliest records of festivals come from ancient Egypt. The Egyptians left descriptions of their lives in the form of beautiful pictures carved in stone. They also wrote details on sheets made of papyrus, a plant which grew along the banks of the Nile.

The feast of Opet

The Nile has been the source of life for Egypt for 5,000 years. Every year the river swells and floods the desert oasis leaving fertile soil for growing crops.

The most important time for festivals was when the flood was at its height. People could not work in the fields so they rested and celebrated their many gods with huge banquets, dancing and processions.

One of the most popular festivals was that held in honour of the God Amon, the chief Egyptian god. Amon was honoured in a huge festival that lasted for twenty-four days.

The statue of Amon was removed from his temple in Karnak and placed in a boat-like shrine. Accompanied by the Pharaoh King and many priests, the god was taken in a grand procession to the banks of the Nile. There, the shrine was put in an enormous boat. Heralded by trumpets, cymbals and tambourines, the colourful *flotilla* made its triumphant journey to the great temple of Luxor in Southern Opet.

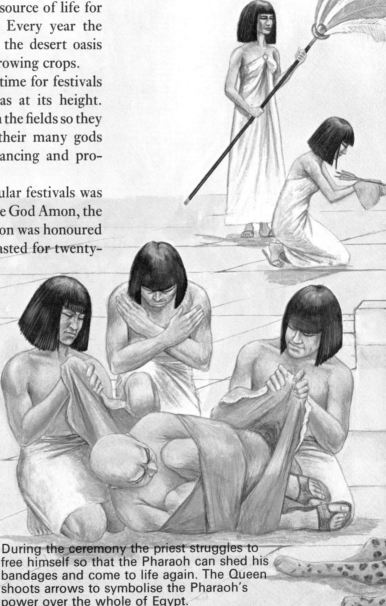

During the ceremony the priest struggles to free himself so that the Pharaoh can shed his bandages and come to life again. The Queen shoots arrows to symbolise the Pharaoh's power over the whole of Egypt.

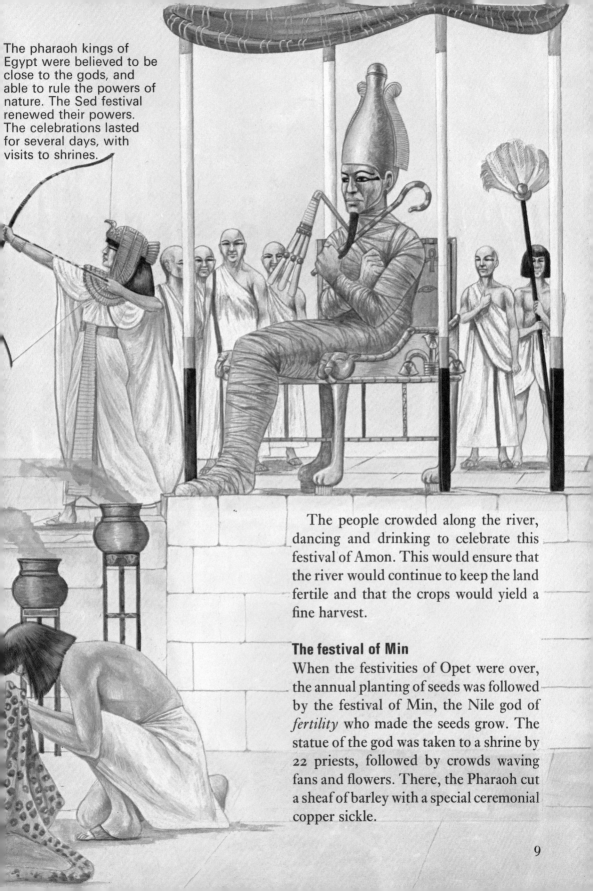

The pharaoh kings of Egypt were believed to be close to the gods, and able to rule the powers of nature. The Sed festival renewed their powers. The celebrations lasted for several days, with visits to shrines.

The people crowded along the river, dancing and drinking to celebrate this festival of Amon. This would ensure that the river would continue to keep the land fertile and that the crops would yield a fine harvest.

The festival of Min

When the festivities of Opet were over, the annual planting of seeds was followed by the festival of Min, the Nile god of *fertility* who made the seeds grow. The statue of the god was taken to a shrine by 22 priests, followed by crowds waving fans and flowers. There, the Pharaoh cut a sheaf of barley with a special ceremonial copper sickle.

9

Greece and Rome

The Gods of ancient Greece were a mighty family of twelve great *deities*. Dionysius, the youngest, was the god of youth, wine and drama. He journeyed round the world like the changing seasons.

In spring, the Greeks honoured Dionysius with a three day wine festival, celebrating birth, life and death. On the first day the jars of new wine were opened and everybody got very drunk. The second day was solemn, the wine was carried to the shrine of the god where it was silently given to everyone over four years old. Day three was devoted to the dead, bowls of a sort of porridge were placed at the shrine of the god *Hermes* who guided the souls of the dead in the underworld.

Fun and games

Drama festivals began as a dance given at a wine festival to thank Dionysius. The first plays told of the adventures of this merry-making god. Drama festivals were

▲ The treading of grapes was a time for celebrations. Much wine was drunk and boys danced upon the grapes to the music of flutes.

▲ Dionysius, god of wine and vegetation. Dionysius was the god of pleasure too, with many festivals in his honour.

◄ This picture, taken from a Greek vase, shows a group of runners taking part in the Olympic pentathlon. The pentathlon consisted of five events: running, long jump, discus and javelin throwing, and wrestling.

very important events, all work stopped so that people could go to the theatre. Masks were used so that people at the back could see the characters in the play, and some actors wore thick boots to make them taller. Since Grecian times, plays, masks, dances and even stilts have remained an important part of festivities.

The Olympic Games

Every four years a great festival was held at *Olympia*, the Olympic Games. People came from all over Greece. The competitions took place amongst the altars of the gods and were followed by great feasts. The winners were awarded garlands of vine leaves and were greatly honoured. Winning meant that you had achieved excellence, and so it pleased the gods. The Olympic games are still a festival of supreme achievement.

The ruins of the Roman theatre at Taormina in Sicily show the huge arena surrounded by seats for thousands of people. ▼

The Romans

Soon after the autumn sowing had been completed, the Romans held a great seven day festival in honour of Saturn, god of harvest. This was the Saturnalia festival which has come to be known as topsy turvy time. The law courts were closed and everybody had a long holiday.

During Saturnalia the slaves were served by their masters. They wore their master's *togas*. People gave each other presents, usually wax candles, and terracotta dolls were given to the children. No wars could be started and no criminal punished during the period of the feast.

The ancient winter merry-making time of pagan Rome was chosen by the Christians for their celebration of Christmas. Following the Roman invasion of Britain, the traditions of Saturnalia were continued in England as part of the Twelfth Night festivities. In the time of Queen Elizabeth the first, twelfth night banquets were held, with lords changing places with servants.

Northern festivals

The Vikings of Scandinavia were a warlike group of tribes who invaded western Europe in the 8th century A.D. The Vikings' most important festival was called Yule. The word has given the English their word yell, for the festival was a great shout to the gods to bring back the sun. This happened in the middle of the long dark and cold Scandinavian winter.

The Yule festivities

The festival of Yule gets its name from the god Jolnir, or Thor, the god of war. Jolnir was chief of the Viking gods, who ruled Valhalla, the home of dead warriors. The Vikings believed that the ghosts of the dead came searching for food from their Yuletide feasts, so they left food and drink for the ghostly visitors.

Great bonfires lit the winter skies, and yule logs were brought into the villages to celebrate the returning spring. The tree represented the returning life after the death of winter. Candles and evergreen leaves representing light and continuing fertility are old Yule traditions which are still part of winter celebrations today.

▲ The God of war, Thor, with his hammer, the symbol of his power. Thor was also worshipped by farmers.

At Christmas time, the yule log was brought in and it blazed in the hearth as a symbol of good fortune for the coming year.

The Celts

Every year, a festival of music, dance and song called Eisteddfod is held in Wales. The people who organise it are the descendants of the Celts of ancient Britain. When Christian people invaded Wales they adopted the language and customs of the Celts. Their legends and rituals have become part of Christian celebrations.

The spring festival of Beltane

Like the Vikings, the Celts divided their year into summer and winter: their festivals included sun worship, sacrifices and songs.

The ancient May festival, called Beltane, was a celebration of the returning summer sun. During the festival, people rolled spinning wheels of fire down the mountains and hills. They lit up great bonfires in holy places and topped them up with the branches of the sacred oak tree. They marked the holy sites by circles of stones. Herds of cattle which provided the Celts with food and skins were driven through the sacred flames. The Celts believed this would keep the animals pure and free from disease. The druids or priests sang praises to the gods while the people danced round the fires. The dances recalled the journey of the circling sun.

▲ This stone figure from Boa Island in Ireland was carved during a period of change from pagan customs and traditions to Christian worship.

During the ancient sun festival of Beltane, the Celts drove their cattle through the flames and danced in honour of the sun. ▼

Winter festivals today

The traditional symbols of winter festivals are fire and light as this is the darkest and coldest time of the year. Many of the customs of the pagan celebrations of winter time are now part of the Christian Christmas. Traditional folk festivals brighten up the hardest season of the year.

St Lucia's Day in Sweden

December the 13th is traditionally the longest and darkest night of the Swedish winter. This is the feast of the martyred Christian, St Lucia of Syracuse. The end of the long night was celebrated for centuries with a candle-lit feast at dawn. In the 19th century it became traditional for the food and drink to be brought in by a figure dressed all in white. Today, hundreds of little girls with crowns of candles lead the St Lucia festivities all over Sweden.

Ring out the old, bring in the new

The end of the year is a time for some of the rowdiest celebrations of winter. From north to south, east to west, people welcome the new year with some very odd customs. This is a new start, a time for new resolutions. People celebrate with noise to chase away the old year, and bells to welcome the new year.

In Denmark, boys collect old china to smash on neighbours' doors. In parts of America and Germany, the old year is shot out with the crack of gunfire.

Scotland

New Year in Scotland is called Hogmanay. The custom of first footing is the most important part of the celebrations. The chimes of midnight are followed by a knock on the door. A dark stranger enters carrying a piece of coal, representing wealth, and a sprig of mistletoe, as a protection from the spirits of the old year. The stranger puts the coal in the fireplace, the mistletoe on the mantelpiece, then everyone shouts 'Happy New Year', and offers the first footer the first of many drinks. In the streets the crowds gather to sing 'Auld Lang Syne' the traditional New Year's song in Scotland.

At New Year in Naples, people throw some pieces of old furniture and rubbish into the street.

▲ The mid-winter fire festival of Up-Helly-Aa in the Shetlands is intended to revive the heat and light of the sun.

Splashing about in the fountains of Trafalgar Square is one way of celebrating the New Year in London. ▶

Spring festivals

The arrival of spring is welcomed with a variety of colourful festivals all over Europe and the world. Many of the customs began in pagan times. Some are the local folk traditions and customs of the people of certain towns and villages. The spring festival in Sweden is called Walpurgis Night with bonfires and traditional spring songs welcoming spring morning.

Bringing spring into the village

In mediaeval times it was traditional on the eve of May the first for the young people to spend the night in the woods and fields outside the village. They also danced and played and gathered branches of blossom and greenery which they brought into the village at dawn. They placed flowers and leaves round the maypole, and laid them at doors and windows.

Today the celebrations are still centred round the maypoles which are decorated with ribbons and flowers. The star of the festival is the May queen who announces spring and is honoured and welcomed by the crowd.

The *morris dancers* are an important part of the English festivities. They perform their five hundred-year-old dances round the maypole. The sound of the morris men's bells and the waving of their white handkerchiefs carry echoes of the past directly into the present day celebrations.

▲ Morris dancers have been known for centuries in England. They perform ritual dances at seasonal fertility festivals.

The cricket festival in Florence

An unusual spring festival is held in Florence in Italy on the fortieth day after Easter. The 'Festa Del Gallo', or cricket festival is a great favourite with Florentine children.

The song of the cricket is a sure sign of spring, so on the Festa Del Gallo, stalls all over Florence sell brightly painted cages containing a chirping cricket. The children carry their cages to the Cascine park where the families celebrate the festival with balloons and games. If the cricket is still chirping when the children go to bed, they believe they will have good luck for the rest of the year.

A maypole dance in England. The maypole is an ancient fertility symbol. It also represents a tree which young people used to get in from the woods on Mayday and adorn with flowers and garlands. It serves as a centre for their dances and is a relic of pagan tree worship. ▶

Summer festivals

June the 21st is midsummer's day, the date of the summer *solstice* when the sun is farthest away from the equator. This is the longest day of the year.

The ancient stone circles of Stonehenge in England have been the scene of a midsummer festival for centuries. Today, hundreds of people gather at Stonehenge to watch the sun rise high up in the sky. The festival is a ritual welcoming of midsummer: people dressed in white robes take part in ceremonies, processions and chanting. (See illustration on page 6.)

The sun gods of Peru

The traditions of sun worship of the Incas of Peru are now great festivals. The most famous is that held at the magnificent temple of the sun at Curzeo. The sun god is represented by a great solid gold plate which fills one wall of the temple.

On the day of the festival, crowds gather to greet the rising sun. As soon as the first rays strike the golden turrets of the temple the people shout a huge welcome which grows louder and louder as the sun lights up the early morning sky to shine in full splendour on the temple. The day continues with magnificent processions, music, dancing and singing ceremonies and festive feasts.

The climax of the day is the ceremony which marks the power of the sun. A priest, carrying a huge polished gold

A reconstruction of the Inca sun festival in Peru today. Processions take place in honour of the sun. ▼

mirror, reflects the burning rays of the sun off the shining metal onto a heap of cotton, which is set alight by the fierce heat of the reflected sun.

▲ Midsummer festival in Sweden. It was originally pagan but was adopted by the church as the Feast of St John the Baptist.

Summer superstitions

In many European countries midsummer festivals celebrate the Christian feast of St John the Baptist, but the rituals still contain the old traditions of ancient times. From Scandinavia, the Netherlands through Germany, France, Spain and Portugal, the bonfires of midsummer light the skies.

The bonfires represent the victory of light over darkness, and people celebrate summer with folk songs and dancing round the flames. It is the traditional festival of love, with many old superstitious customs still being observed for fun. In Portugal, girls put three beans under their pillow, in the hope that they will see the face of their future husband in their dreams. In Sweden, girls pick nine different kinds of flowers and hide them under the pillow. In France, couples hold hands and jump over the dying embers of the bonfires.

Autumn festivals

Mellow and fruitful autumn is the time for harvesting or gathering in the crops. In England, the harvest home is still a popular festival. Gifts of fruit and vegetables are placed around the church altars for a special harvest service in thanksgiving for a good crop. After the service the gifts are given to needy people in the community. Autumn represents the slow dying of the year and the harvesting of food for the coming winter.

Corn dollies

In mediaeval times shortages of food were common in many countries, so not surprisingly farmers did everything they could to ensure a good crop. The corn dolly is still part of many harvest celebrations. At harvest time little corn figures were woven from the last corn gathered, and then placed on the altars at the harvest service. The dolly is a symbol of continuing good harvests. The figures were believed to bring life to the new seeds which would provide the next year's crop.

▲ A rice dolly from Melanesia made with the last of the harvested crop.

▲ 'Sukkot' is a Jewish harvest festival. Festivities are held in little shelters called sukkas built to symbolise the wanderings of the families' forefathers. The huts are decorated with harvest fruit and flowers.

The return from the pastures

In Germany and Switzerland, September is the traditional month for shepherds and cowherds to return from their mountain pastures. This is the occasion for celebrations in the Alpine villages. The animals are decorated with flowers, and villagers, dressed in national costumes, turn out to welcome the shepherds home. In the evening the villagers enjoy a celebration meal, followed by folk singing and dancing.

The Munich Beer festival

The Oktoberfest of Munich on the third Sunday in October is a special harvest festival in Germany. It celebrates the hop harvest from which the Germans make their much-loved beer. On that day there are fairs, parades and pageants. Every seven years the men who make the beer barrels perform their traditional five hundred-year-old dance, called the Coopers dance.

◄ The first juice of the grapes is pressed at Manilla in Spain and the wine harvest festival is all set up to take place.

Hallowe'en

Hallow is an old English word which means holy. 'All-Hallow-Even' meant the eve of the Christian feast of All Saints. This has now become shortened to the word 'Hallowe'en'.

The feast of All Saints, when the souls of the faithful are honoured and remembered, falls on November the 1st. The church chose this day as the people were accustomed to remembering the dead at this time of year. The pre-Christian traditions were full of ghosts and witches and fear of the dark. In Celtic Britain, November the first was not only the first day of winter, but also the first day of the new year.

Hallowe'en today is a mixture of all the old customs. The bonfires are now lit on November the fifth in England to celebrate Guy Fawkes' attempt to blow up the Houses of Parliament. In other countries the fires light the Hallowe'en celebrations.

Witches and ghosts

Witches and ghosts are now just part of Hallowe'en fun, but for hundreds of years the witch and her broomstick were taken very seriously. People believed that witches were friends of the evil spirits which wandered about at Hallowe'en.

The tradition of wearing masks at Hallowe'en began as a way to frighten the witches and spirits away. Scottish children now wear masks and dress up like ghosts, which they call ghoulies and kelpies, and knock on doors to ask for nuts and apples and money.

Trick or Treat

In the United States and Canada, children have the same tradition, which they call trick or treat. Carrying lanterns, and dressed like witches and ghosts in orange and black, the traditional Hallowe'en colours, the children go from door to door threatening to trick their neighbours if they are not treated to the traditional sweets wrapped in orange and black paper. After running round the streets the children return home for their Hallowe'en parties.

▲ Dressing up as a witch is part of the fun of Hallowe'en.

▲ To play bobbing for apples a tub is filled up with water, with apples floating in it. Children with hands tied up try to grasp an apple with their teeth.

Hallowe'en lantern. ▲

Apples and apple games

Bobbing apples and swinging apples are two traditional games for Hallowe'en. The apples float in bowls of water or swing on the ends of string. The aim of the game is to take a bite of the apple without using your hands. Apple games began because the Celts believed that the silver branches of the apple tree helped dead souls to pass into their heaven, which they called Avalon. The Romans roasted apples in huge fires at their winter feast of Pomona.

Lanterns

Turnips and swedes are part of winter's crop and are now used to light Hallowe'en parties. The inside of the vegetable is hollowed out and slits made in it to represent eyes, nose and mouth. A candle is then put inside the vegetable lantern, so that the eerie face can light the celebrations.

Children playing 'Trick or Treat'! ▼

23

Jewish festivals

The Jewish faith is based on the belief that the one true God has chosen the Jews as His people. He has given them instructions in the Torah which is the heart of the Jewish scriptures. The Christians call this book the Old Testament.

Rosh Hashanah

Rosh Hashanah is the Jewish New Year. 1981 is the year 5741 for the Jews. The people celebrate God's creation of the world, and remember the bible story of *Abraham*. The new year is a time of ten day's *penitence*, when Jews examine their relationship with God, whom they believe is their judge. It is traditional to eat an apple dipped in honey to symbolise the fruitful new year.

The festival of Shavuot celebrates the fruitfulness of the Promised Land. This is the time when first fruits are picked. ▼

Passover or Pesach

The Passover is the Jewish spring festival which lasts for eight days, when the people remember how their ancestors escaped from slavery in Egypt. On the first night of Pesach, families get together for a special feast called the Seder feast. A traditional meal of lamb, roasted eggs, apples, nuts, bitter herbs and watercress is served on beautiful Seder dishes, accompanied by *unleavened bread*. The youngest member of the family asks four traditional questions, the answers to which tell the story of Haggadah: the freeing of Israel, home of the Jews.

The first and last two days of the festival are official religious holidays when shops, offices and schools are closed.

The feast of Purim

Purim, one of the liveliest festivals, celebrates the saving of the Jews from a plot to kill them, as told in the Bible story of Esther.

▲ During the Purim festival, in Israel, little girls dress up as Esther and street processions include colourful floats and dance troupes.

A young Jewish boy holds Chanukkah candles, one for each day of the eight-day Light festival which celebrates every Jew's right to his own faith or beliefs. ▼

A day of *fasting* is held before the feast day. On the feast itself there are great processions, with hundreds of little girls dressed up as the holy Esther. Families meet for a reading of the bible story.

Chanukkah

Chanukkah celebrates Jewish religious education and the story of the miraculous lighting of candles in the temple of Jerusalem by *Judas Maccabeus*. A festival of light, Chanukkah is the time when every Jewish home is lit with eight candles, for each of the eight days of the festival. There are lots of parties for the children, and people give each other gifts.

▲ Jesus Christ was born in Bethlehem nearly two thousand years ago. This was the first Christmas morning.

In Brittany, France, festivals called 'pardons' are held in honour of the saints. ▼

Christian feasts

The Christian festivals are based on the story of Jesus, whose teachings are followed by millions of people all over the world. Christmas and Easter are the most widely observed festivals. Most Christian festivals are a celebration of events in the life of Christ.

The Epiphany

The Epiphany is the sixth of January, and recalls the day when the three Kings followed the star of Bethlehem and arrived at the stable where Jesus was born. In Italy, children receive their Christmas presents on the eve of Epiphany. They believe that their gifts are brought by a lady called La Befana.

The story of La Befana tells how this little lady refused to leave her housework and follow the three Kings when they came by. When she had finished her sweeping, she tried to find her way to the stable, but she lost her way. She is still supposed to be roaming the world looking for the baby Jesus, and passes through Italy on the feast of Epiphany, leaving presents for all the children.

Pentecost

Forty days after Easter, Jesus left the twelve apostles, and for a time they were confused and bewildered, and unable to teach. While praying on the feast of Pentecost, they all felt a tremendous spirit which encouraged them to spread the teachings of Jesus. The feast is known as Whitsun as it was a traditional day for baptising converts, who were always dressed in white. Whitsun is the official birthday of the Christian Church.

Saints' Days

Most Christian countries have their patron saints, who are remembered on their feast days. For instance St David, patron Saint of Wales, is honoured on the first of March.

A Palm Sunday procession in Italy. It celebrates Jesus's entry into Jerusalem when people waved palms to greet him. ▶

Christmas

Christmas is the celebration of the birth of Jesus Christ. The story of Christmas tells how Jesus was born in a stable at Bethlehem, where the baby and his parents, Mary and Joseph, were visited by shepherds and later by the three wise men known traditionally as the three Kings.

For all Christians, the most important part of Christmas is the church service. At midnight on Christmas Eve, the bells ring out all over the world. Inside the churches, candles light the little cribs which illustrate the Christmas story. Christmas is the time when people get together, and have a feast and exchange gifts.

▲ Singing carols round the tree began in the last century. The word carol means a ring dance or song.

In Mexico, a 'piñata' or bird filled up with sweets is smashed by a blindfolded child. ▼

Christmas past and present

The Christmas celebrations take place at the same time as the ancient pagans held their mid-winter festivities. Many of the old *traditions* are still part of the Christian festival.

The traditional winter scenes on Christmas cards tend to make people forget that for half the world, Christmas comes at the height of summer. In Australia, and many other countries, the Christmas feast is eaten on beaches, or at summer picnics. In spite of this, the old northern traditions are still part of Christmas in the South.

Christmas traditions

Holly, mistletoe and the Christmas tree all play a part in Christmas traditions. Holly has been part of winter celebrations since Roman times. The berries symbolise the blood of Christ. When it is used

as a decoration, it represents eternal life and hospitality.

A family celebrating Christmas in Bethlehem, Israel.

Mistletoe

Mistletoe grows in old trees and was a sacred plant of the druids. It grew on the sacred oak tree and stayed green when the leaves of the oak fell in winter. Because the berries grow in pairs, mistletoe has come to stand for undying love.

The Christmas tree

The Christmas tree has been part of German Christmases since the 16th century. When Queen Victoria married Prince Albert, a German, he brought the tradition to England. Now millions and millions of trees are decorated all over the world with candles, fairy lights and glittering ornaments.

The Christmas feast

The turkey is an American tradition, which became popular in England at the beginning of the 20th century. Before this, the traditional Christmas meat was a boar's head, or a rack of beef. The Christmas pudding used to be a sort of old English porridge which became a figgy pudding and today is a delicious mixture of dried fruits, eggs, flour, suet and brandy. It is traditional to put a piece of holly on the top, and set the pudding alight before carrying it to the table. This ritual comes from the ancient Celtic sun-worshipping festival. The flaming pudding tells the guests that winter will end and the sun will return.

Easter

In pre-Christian times Easter was the feast of the pagan goddess of spring, who was called Eostre. Today this great feast is held to remember the crucifixion and resurrection of Jesus Christ who was nailed to the cross and died on the day that is now called Good Friday. All over the world people attend solemn church services at three o'clock in the afternoon. The services tell the story of the stations of the cross: the events that happened on the way to a hill called Calvary. This is where Christ was crucified.

Easter Sunday

This is the day when Christians believe Christ rose from the dead, showing that He is the son of God, so Easter day is a very happy day. After church services, people celebrate this event, and the end of the sad time of Lent. Now is the time for feasting.

Easter eggs

Eggs are the traditional symbol for new life. In rising from the dead, Christians believe that Christ showed to them that there is a life after death for everyone.

There are many folk stories surrounding the receiving of eggs, and children have their own Easter egg rituals.

In France the children believe that the eggs are brought by the Easter bells that ring out on Easter morning, and leave the eggs hidden under bushes and on the branches of trees. In most countries it is the hare, or Easter rabbit which brings the eggs, and in Germany the children put out little nests of moss, so that the rabbit can leave the eggs safe from harm.

The Easter rabbit, like the egg, is a symbol of the fertility of spring. As the spring crops hide in the earth, so the rabbit hides in his burrow.

Egg games

Decorating eggs, rolling eggs, and knocking eggs are all popular customs still practised today. In the White House in Washington, USA, eggs are rolled across the green lawns in a competition to see who can roll eggs the farthest.

The drama of Christ's sufferings is re-enacted in a Passion play at Oberammergau in Austria. ▶

Indian children in Northern Mexico daub themselves with white spots which symbolise Christ's blood. ▼

In Scotland and in Australia children knock eggs in clenched fists and have egg races in a game called pace egging.

The Easter tree

In Sweden, it has been a custom for branches of trees to be brought into the house so that they will blossom on Easter Sunday. This has led to the custom of the Easter tree. Branches and twigs are decorated with little wooden eggs, and real eggs are blown and decorated with many beautiful designs. There are hundreds of decorated eggs in folk museums all over the world. The tradition of egg decorating is hundreds of years old. It is an attractive custom for both children and adults and it is easy to do.

Muslim festivals

The founder of the religion of Islam was a man called Mohammed. The followers of Islam are called Muslims. Muslims lead their lives according to the teachings which are written in a book, called the Qur'an, or Koran. The rules of Islam instruct Muslims to fast, to give alms to the poor and to devote their life to God. They must pray five times a day, and make a pilgrimage to the holy city of Mecca at least once in a lifetime.

The lunar calendar
The Muslim calendar is based on the movements of the moon. The year is eleven days shorter than the years based on the movements of the sun, so the festive days change from year to year.

Meelad al nabi
Muslims celebrate the birthday of Mohammed with readings from the Qur'an. The story of the prophet's life is told in homes and mosques.

Ramadan
The month of Ramadan is very important to Muslims. It is a time of very strict fasting during the hours of daylight, when Muslims are forbidden to eat, drink or smoke. Much of the time is spent in prayer. The rules are strictly obeyed, so that every Muslim can learn self-discipline, and experience poverty. The end of the month is marked by a festival called Id al fitr, which means small festival.

Id al fitr
Id al fitr is the most popular festival in the Muslim calendar, coming at the end of the harsh month of Ramadan. At sunrise everybody bathes and puts on new clothes, even the very poor find something new to wear. Dressed in their new clothes, Muslims go to the mosque for

the first prayers of the day. Id al fitr celebrations resemble the Christian Christmas in many ways. As people leave the mosque they wish each other a happy day and leave to join their families for a celebration meal. People give each other gifts. The children receive sweets, money, presents, and special id al fitr cards.

Pilgrimage to Mecca

A visit to Mecca is the most important event in a Muslim's life. Every year millions of people travel to this holy city which has been a shrine since the time of Abraham, and where Mohammed himself was born. In Mecca, the pilgrim is expected to visit the Ka'aba. This is a huge cube-shaped building. In one corner is a black stone surrounded by silver. Mohammed declared the Ka'aba to be the shrine of the one true god, whom Muslims call Allah.

Id al adha

The month of pilgrimage is an important festival for all Muslims which ends in a four-day feast called Id al adha. It is the traditional festival of sacrifice. Families club together to buy a sheep or cow, which is then killed according to Islamic law, cooked and divided between the families, their friends and the poor.

Muslims are dancing to celebrate the end of fasting which also marks the end of Ramadan. ▶

◀ Crowds of people gather for prayers at the end of Ramadan in Kano, Northern Nigeria.

Hindu festivals

In India, the year is one long series of festivals. All the great religions have their followers with their own beliefs and celebrations. The Hindu religion, with 453 million followers has many important feasts, as do the religions of the Sikh, Jain and Parsee religions.

Hinduism

The Hindus believe that everything in the world is constantly changing. There is only one thing that does not change. This is a state of being or soul which they call Brahman. For Hindus all living things contain a part of Brahman, without it nothing would exist. They hope to become part of Brahman although this cannot happen within a life time. They worship Brahman in the form of many gods.

A Hindu girl ties the sacred Raksha bandhan thread on her brother's wrist. It is a symbol of the bond between them. ▼

Raksha Bandhan

The family is very important to Hindus. One of the loveliest festivals is the family festival called Raksha Bandhan. On this day, sisters weave a silk bracelet of red and gold thread, which they tie ceremonially on the wrists of their brothers. The bracelet represents the bond between brothers and sister: she shows her love for him by making this gift, and in return, by wearing the bracelet, he promises to protect her forever. The festival is based on an old legend which tells how the god Indra was protected from demons by a silk bracelet called a rakhi, which was given to him by his wife.

Diwali

In October or November the Hindus welcome Lakshi, the goddess of wealth. Every home is decorated with little lamps, called divas, and patterns of rice flour decorate the doorsteps. Lights are also lit in temples and streets. Diwali is the beginning of the business year, and also marks the sowing of the winter crop.

Dusshera

The important festival of Dusshera in the autumn celebrates the triumph of good over evil. The festival lasts for ten days, and tells the story of the goddess Durga, the war goddess. Durga helped the sun hero, Rama, to slay the evil demon King Ravana.

On the day of the festival, giant figures of the demon gods are filled with fireworks and explosives. They are set alight by arrows of fire, shot from the bow of a figure dressed as the hero Rama. In the town of Mysore great processions of elephants parade through the city streets.

In the north of India the battles of Rama and Ravana are acted out on great floats which are driven through the city.

Holi

Holi is a celebration of the love of the god Krishna for a girl called Radha. It celebrates the arrival of the spring flowers. Holi lasts for five days, and is known as the festival of colour. People buy red powder and coloured water to throw over each other. There are processions, bonfires and dancing, while statues of the gods are carried round the streets on enormous floats.

The car festivals

Cars are enormous floats which carry the shrines of the gods in many Indian festivals, the most famous being the car festival in a town called Puri. The shrine of the god Jaganath is in the temple of Puri, and once a year it is carried through the streets on a great car, dragged by teams of men. People come from all over the countryside to watch the colourful procession.

▲ During the Hindu autumn festival of lights or Diwali little clay oil lamps flicker throughout India.

China and Japan

The folk festivals of Japan and China began thousands of years ago. The Chinese and Japanese have, a great respect for their ancestors and for the past. Ritual and tradition are an important part of every day life.

Following the revolution on mainland China, the government and the people felt, for many years, that money usually spent on festivals should be used on more important things. In recent years festivals have become popular again as a way of getting together to keep traditions alive. In Hong Kong, Singapore, and every other place where groups of Chinese people have settled, festivals draw crowds because of their colour and gaiety.

The Chinese New Year

The Chinese New Year usually falls between mid-January and mid-February, because the Chinese base their year on the *lunar calendar*. The celebrations begin on the stroke of midnight with fire crackers exploding in the street to frighten away the spirits of the old year. Each year has the name of an animal. There are twelve names which make the cycle of years: the rat, ox, tiger, hare, dragon, snake, horse, sheep, monkey, cockerel, dog and pig. 1980 is the year of the monkey.

Throughout the celebrations many people wear masks of the year's animal. Hundreds and thousands of lanterns and flags decorate the streets and houses. Families gather together to eat special food. The children's favourite, Yuan-Hsiae, is a new year dumpling made with rice, flour, walnuts and almonds.

People give each other presents, and go together to watch the brightly-coloured dances of the lions and dragons.

Japanese festivals

On New Year's day, after a visit to their local shrine, families visit friends and neighbours. The children play the traditional new year game of battledore and shuttlecock. The battledores are beautifully decorated carved paddle-like bats, which are decorated with flowers or pictures of favourite pop and sporting stars. Some of the battledores are old and all are prized possessions.

◀ Dragon dancers leading a New Year procession in Singapore. The dragon is a divine king in Chinese legends, and thousands of dragons dance in the streets at the New Year.

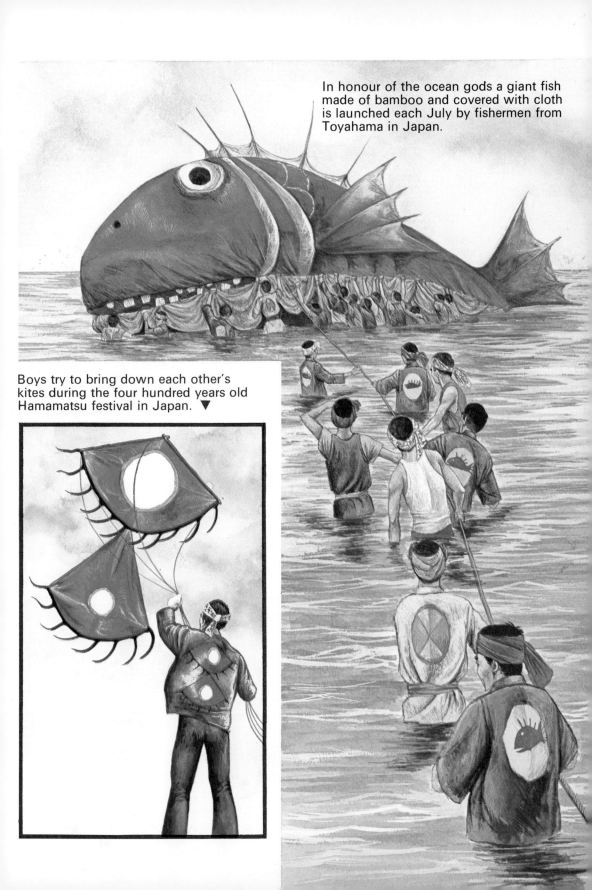

In honour of the ocean gods a giant fish made of bamboo and covered with cloth is launched each July by fishermen from Toyahama in Japan.

Boys try to bring down each other's kites during the four hundred years old Hamamatsu festival in Japan. ▼

Children's festivals

All festivals are enjoyed by young people, but there are some festivals which especially belong to the children. Hina Matsuri in Japan and the tree planting festivals in Israel are two examples.

Hina Matsuri
March the third is Hina Matsuri, or Girl's Doll festival, which is about 1,000 years old. Every family has a collection of old traditional dolls which are handed down from daughter to daughter. At Hina Matsuri these dolls are formally displayed for a week.

At the end of the festival, children make dolls of paper and cloth; they place them in straw baskets and set them afloat on the rivers, to be swept away, according to tradition, to another world.

Tree planting in Israel
In Israel, the second of February is the annual tree planting festival for children. On this day Israeli children plant trees in the forests and give money for trees. The ceremonial tree planting recalls the story in the Talmud, which says that their Jewish ancestors planted trees when their children were born. When the children grew up, the trunks of the trees were used to make their wedding canopies or tents.

◀ Young boys dressed up for the bun festival which takes place on a small island near Hong Kong. Towers of buns are built for the occasion and boys run up the ladders to try to get them down.

On Kamakura Day, a snow festival in Japan, children build a special snow cave, where they play and offer apples and nuts to adult visitors. ▶

Africa

The continent of Africa contains over two thousand tribes. Many Africans follow one or other of the major world religions, and celebrate the festivals of Islam or Christianity. Other Africans follow the traditional tribal beliefs and worship gods in many different ways.

Every tribe worships a supreme being; some honour one god, others honour many gods. These spirits may be ancestors, or the spirits of the sun, moon, thunder or rain. Festivals strengthen the ties between the people of the tribe. They are an occasion for acting out ancient customs and rituals which play a very essential part in keeping the tribe together.

Every December, the ruler of the Ebo tribe in Nigeria is presented to the people. This is the occasion for the Offala festival and for much merry-making activities. ▼

The Egungun festival

The traditions of the Yoruba tribe in south-western Nigeria are still observed in a major religious festival in honour of the spirits of ancient ancestors called the Egungun. According to tradition these spirits control the lives of the living, and must be respected and honoured.

Their great festival takes place in early June. Following a night of prayer people crowd to the town. The distant sound of drums grows louder and louder, heralding the arrival of the Egungun. These are masqueraders, people dressed up as the spirits of the ancestors. Their brightly coloured costumes are topped by wooden masks. Each of the ancestors is immediately recognisable to the thousands of spectators lining the streets. The drums accompany the dances of the spirits as they go in procession to receive a blessing.

This religious festival in honour of the Egungun is also a thanksgiving for the harvest. Corn pap, yams and bean cakes

are placed on the Egungun shrines. For a whole week the dancing and festivities continue. The festival is an acting out of the basic beliefs and traditions of the Yoruba people.

The yam festival

Yams are sweet potatoes, which are as important in the African diet as bread or rice. The yam festival is a traditional harvest festival in many parts of Africa.

In Ghana, for 40 days before the festival begins, no yams are brought into the markets. The farmers stay in their villages to supervise the harvest. The best yams are put aside to offer to the god of the harvest.

On the day of the festival, the yams are brought to the towns. Everybody dresses up in their best clothes, or in traditional costumes to join the great procession which weaves its way through the streets. After the procession there are great celebration parties. People dance, sing, eat and drink wine made of palms.

Independence days

For decades many parts of Africa were colonised, which meant that Africans were ruled by people from other lands. This century has seen the Africans taking control of their own affairs. Independence day celebrations are now important festivals, with masks, fantastic costumes, ancient tribal dances and traditional music.

The Berber Fantasia is a festival held every year by Berber tribesmen in North Africa. A fair is set up and people such as acrobats and jugglers come and entertain the crowds. ▶

The annual West Indian Londoners' carnival.

Carnivals

The word carnival is used to describe the merrymaking, processions and amusement that take place during a festival. Carnival was originally an old Italian festival which lasted from Twelfth Night to Ash Wednesday. This period before Lent is called Shrovetide, which is the traditional time for people to 'let their hair down' before the sad weeks of Lent.

In England, Shrovetide is celebrated on Shrove Tuesday or Pancake day, the day before Ash Wednesday. It is the traditional day for eating and tossing pancakes. In many towns there are pancake races, with the competitors running through the streets, tossing their pancakes as they go.

The traditions of carnivals today
Carnivals are folk festivals, when people wear their national costumes, and enjoy performing traditional dances, plays and music. Many carnivals are famous events drawing tourists from all over the world.

In Mexico and Brazil, the colourful South American carnivals are planned months ahead. Great floats carry actors performing plays about bandits, and the triumph of good over evil. In Spain where carnival is called fiesta time, there are long processions of people dressed in masks and elaborate costumes. Guitars and castanets accompany public dancing all over the country.

In New Orleans, in the USA, the carnival is called Mardi Gras, or fat Tuesday, with jazz bands, floats and horseback parades. In Nice, in southern France, King Carnival leads the celebrations accompanied by his court of clowns. Carnivals brighten up the dreary months of winter, before the brighter days of spring.

Carnival in Trinidad
West Indian carnivals are famous throughout the world. Throughout the West Indies the music of steel bands fills the air at Carnival time. For months before the festival, people work very hard making hundreds of exotic, elaborate costumes to wear in the processions.

Giant characters are paraded during a
town carnival in Austria.

Books to read

Festivals and Celebrations, Roland Auget; Franklin Watts 1975
European Folk Festivals, Sam Epstien and Beryl Epstien; Garrard Publishing Co. 1968
Customs and Holidays Around the World, Lavinia Dobler; Fleet Press 1962
Holidays Around the World, Joseph Gaer; Little, Brown 1953
The Holiday Book, Martin Greif; Universe Books 1978
Holidays and Festivals, Charles Chavel; Shulsinger Brothers 1956
All About American Holidays, Maymie R. Krythe; Harper and Row 1962
How Holidays Happened, Lucy G. Thompson; Horizon Publishers and Distributors 1976

Things to do

Make a calendar of the festivals you celebrate. Read the legends of other countries.

Look up the stories mentioned in this book. The stories behind the beliefs of Jewish people and Christians can be found in the Bible. The stories of the Greeks and Egyptians can be found in books of myths.

Make a battledore and shuttlecock. You will find pictures in books about old games. Decorate them, like Japanese children do.

Help an adult to make a festive meal from another country. There are lots of international cookery books with the recipes for traditional festive foods.

Make a list of all the things that people all over the world have in common when they celebrate. If you have friends from abroad, ask them how they celebrate festivals at home. Ask your grandparents what they used to do at Easter and Christmas when they were little.

Places to go

If you live near a temple, church, mosque, or synagogue, ask if you can visit there at the time of a festival.

Go to your local museum, and see what they have to tell you about festivals at home and abroad.

Visit your local travel agent and see if they have pictures of celebrations in other countries.

If you are in New York, you might want to visit the United Nations, where you can find out a lot about people in different countries.

Glossary

Here is a list of some of the special words used in this book.

Abraham: The bible says that Abraham lived 4,000 years ago. An ancestor of the Jews, he is honoured by both Jews and Christians.

Deities: Gods.

Fasting: Going without food and drink.

Fertility: Fruitfulness, fertile earth is earth which produces good crops.

Flotilla: A fleet of ships.

Hermes: Messenger of the Greek gods.

Judas Maccabeus: He led a rebellion against King Antiochus IV in the 2nd century BC (before Christ).

Lunar calendar: A calendar based on the regular movements of the moon.

Martyr: Someone who dies for what he believes.

Morris dance: An ancient Spanish dance brought to England by the Moors, and popular in English spring festivities since mediaeval times.

Olympia: The Greek city where the first Olympic games were held in 776 BC.

Pagans: A Christian name for ancient peoples who were not Christians.

Penitence: Showing regret at having sinned.

Pilgrimage: A journey to a holy shrine.

Sacrifice: An offering to God.

Saints: Very holy people.

Solstice: The two occasions in the year when the sun is farthest away from the equator.

Symbol: Something that represents something else, a sign for some-thing.

Toga: A Greek and Roman man's tunic.

Tradition: A belief or custom passed down from generation to generation.

Unleavened bread: Bread that is baked without yeast.

Index

Illustrations appear in bold type.

46